333.78   Dawson
Daw
        Park naturalist

DATE DUE

CAREER EXPLORATION

Park Naturalist

by Jim Dawson

Consultant:
Tim Merriman
Executive Director
National Association for Interpretation (NAI)

CAPSTONE BOOKS
an imprint of Capstone Press
Mankato, Minnesota

Capstone Books are published by Capstone Press
P.O. Box 669, 151 Good Counsel Drive, Mankato, Minnesota 56002
http://www.capstone-press.com

Library of Congress Cataloging-in-Publication Data
Dawson, Jim, 1949–
    Park Naturalist/by Jim Dawson.
    p.cm.—(Career exploration)
    Includes bibliographical references (p. 45) and index.
    Summary: An introduction to the career of park naturalist, including discussion
of educational requirements, duties, workplace, salary, employment outlook, and
possible future positions.
    ISBN 0-7368-0332-7
    1. Natural History—Vocational guidance—Juvenile literature. 2. Park
naturalists—Juvenile literature. [1. Natural history—Vocational guidance. 2. Park
naturalists. 3. Vocational guidance.] I. Title. II. Series.
QH49.D28 2000
333.78'3'023—dc21   99-30637
                                                                                        CIP

Editorial Credits
Matt Doeden, editor; Steve Christensen, cover designer; Kia Bielke, illustrator;
    Heidi Schoof, photo researcher

Photo Credits
Index Stock Imagery/Stephen G. Maka, 36, 41; Steve Chambers, 38
Inga Spence/TOM STACK & ASSOCIATES, 24
International Stock/Jay Thomas, 10
James P. Rowan, 35
J. Lotter/TOM STACK & ASSOCIATES, 9
John Elk III, 18, 27, 30, 33
John Gerlach/TOM STACK & ASSOCIATES, 22
Photri-Microstock/M. Simpson, cover
Shaffer Photography/James L. Shaffer, 13
Transparencies, Inc./Les Saucier, 6; J. Faircloth, 42
Unicorn Stock Photos/Joel Dexter, 15; Karen M. Mullen, 20
Visuals Unlimited/Tim Hauf, 16

Table of Contents

Career Title	Park naturalist
O*NET Number	24302E
DOT Cluster (Dictionary of Occupational Titles)	Professional, technical, and managerial occupations
DOT Number	049.127-010
GOE Number (Guide for Occupational Exploration)	11.07.03
NOC Number (National Occupational Classification-Canada)	2121
Salary Range (U.S. Bureau of Labor Statistics and Human Resources Development Canada, late 1990s figures)	U.S.: $16,000 to $70,000 Canada: $8,500 to $56,300 (Canadian dollars)
Minimum Educational Requirements	U.S.: bachelor's degree Canada: bachelor's degree
Certification/Licensing Requirements	U.S.: none Canada: none

Subject Knowledge

Administration and management; biology; geography; education; English language; fine arts; history and archeology; communications and media; forestry; recreation

Personal Abilities/Skills

Deal with all kinds of people; change activities frequently; plan and direct programs and the activities of others

Job Outlook

U.S.: average growth
Canada: average growth

Personal Interests

Leading-Influencing: interest in leading and influencing others through activities involving high level verbal or numerical abilities

Similar Types of Jobs

Park ranger; interpreter; forester; environmental scientist; conservation scientist; recreation planner

Chapter 1

Park Naturalist

Park naturalists teach people about nature. They teach people about animals, plants, rocks, and other parts of nature. Park naturalists show people how plants and animals live together in their environments. They also help people understand why it is important to protect nature.

Most park naturalists work in nature parks. These include state and national parks. Others work in wildlife preserves, forest preserves, and wildlife refuges. These are safe places for wildlife. People are not allowed to hunt animals in these places.

Park naturalists study nature. They learn how plants and animals live in nature. Park naturalists study the wildlife in parks, forests,

Park naturalists teach people about nature.

and preserves. They learn how parks change with the seasons.

Research

Park naturalists spend much of their time doing research on the wildlife in parks. Research is the close study of a subject. Park naturalists learn about all the different plants and animals in the parks. They learn how plants and animals depend on one another. This helps park naturalists understand problems that might arise in their parks. For example, animals may starve if plants do not get enough water to grow.

Most park naturalists are government employees. State, province, or federal governments create and operate most wildlife preserves and nature parks. These governments often hire park naturalists. Government officials may ask the park naturalists to do research in nature parks. Park naturalists may research population levels of certain animals in an area. Governments

Park naturalists study plants and animals in nature.

may use this research to keep track of endangered species. These species are in danger of dying out.

Park naturalists may set up hiking trails in nature parks. They first learn about the parks. They research the best areas for hiking. They search for safe areas that allow people to see many different plants and animals.

Park naturalists also may teach classes about nature. They may teach classes about wildflowers during spring. They must research all the wildflowers in their area before they can teach these classes. Park naturalists also may set up nature hikes to teach people about the changing seasons. They research the best times during fall to view trees with red, orange, and yellow leaves.

Some park naturalists teach students how to research and study nature. They may use computers and the Internet to help students do research. Students who have to do nature reports may contact park naturalists. Park naturalists may tell these students about nature

Park naturalists may lead nature hikes.

and how to study it. They also may direct students to other sources of information.

Information and Communication

Park naturalists must be good communicators. They use their communication skills to teach others.

Many park naturalists have information on the wildlife in their areas. They may be in charge of libraries, exhibits, or nature centers. The public can learn about nature in these places. Park naturalists may keep track of books in their libraries. They may set up exhibits in nature centers.

Some park naturalists are responsible for Internet sites. These sites include information about nature parks. The sites may list park information such as park hours or special exhibits. Internet sites also may provide information about park wildlife.

Park naturalists may be in charge of other public services. They may answer questions sent through the mail. They may write articles for newspapers or park newsletters. Some park

Park naturalists may teach nature classes.

naturalists arrange awareness activities. These activities may include appearances on TV or radio programs. Park naturalists may talk about wildlife and their habitats on these programs. Habitats are the natural places and conditions in which plants and animals live.

Work Environment

Park naturalists' work environments vary. They do some work indoors. But they spend most of their workday outside. Their work environments depend on where they work. For example, park naturalists who work in northern Canada and Alaska work in cold environments. Park naturalists in Florida's Everglades National Park work in hot and damp environments.

Park naturalists often work alone. Some wildlife preserves and nature parks have more than one park naturalist. But many parks and preserves are small. Park naturalists at these parks and preserves may not have any help.

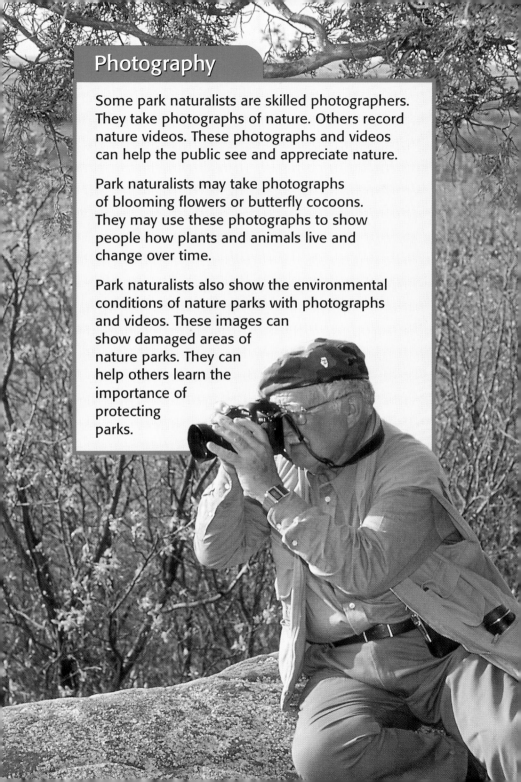

Photography

Some park naturalists are skilled photographers. They take photographs of nature. Others record nature videos. These photographs and videos can help the public see and appreciate nature.

Park naturalists may take photographs of blooming flowers or butterfly cocoons. They may use these photographs to show people how plants and animals live and change over time.

Park naturalists also show the environmental conditions of nature parks with photographs and videos. These images can show damaged areas of nature parks. They can help others learn the importance of protecting parks.

Chapter 2

A Day on the Job

Park naturalists' daily duties depend on their work environments. For example, park naturalists who work in deserts may measure rainfall each day. Park naturalists who work near oceans may keep track of pollution levels. Park naturalists in forest areas may check trees for diseases.

Morning

Many park naturalists check their schedules at the beginning of each day. They note any appointments they may have. For example, park naturalists may lead nature hikes or teach classes. They also may prepare nature centers and other public areas for the day.

Park naturalists' daily duties depend on their work environments.

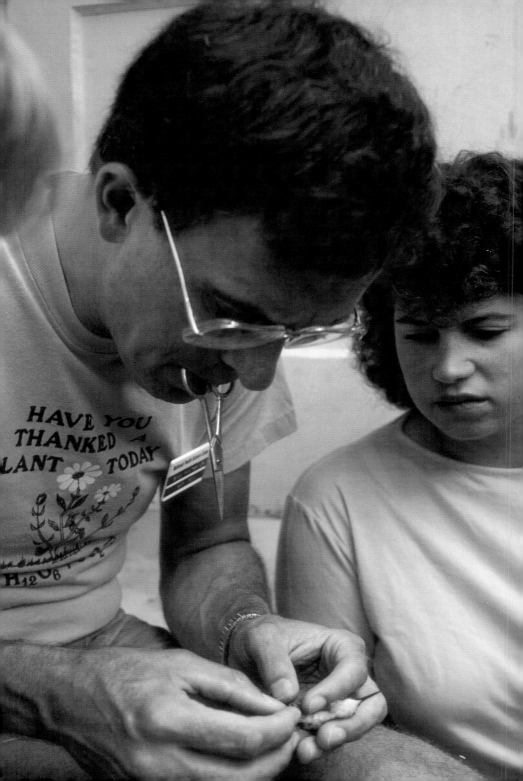

Park naturalists are responsible for people's safety in nature parks. They may check hiking trails and other public areas for safety. They make sure trails are safe and clearly marked. They check for items such as fallen rocks and logs on the trails.

Park naturalists also may check on park wildlife. They may keep track of animal populations. This is especially true for endangered species. For example, park naturalists may check eagle nests for young. This helps park naturalists learn whether eagle populations are increasing.

Afternoon

Park naturalists often work with the public in the afternoon. They may show and explain exhibits in nature centers and other public areas. They also may teach classes.

Park naturalists sometimes lead nature hikes. People who take these hikes may watch birds during spring or summer. During fall, park naturalists may lead hikes to see leaves

Park naturalists teach members of the public through classes and exhibits.

that have turned colors. Park naturalists often bring hikers to the best viewing areas. Park naturalists point out items of interest and answer questions.

Evening

Park naturalists may have to close parks in the evening. They make sure everyone has left the public areas of the park. They lock nature centers and other public areas. They may have to lock gates on park exits.

Park naturalists may work some evenings and nights. They may lead nature hikes that show people nocturnal animals such as bats. Nocturnal animals are active at night. Park naturalists also may give nature presentations after dark. These presentations are called campfire programs.

Park naturalists may help nature hikers view butterflies and other insects.

Chapter 3

The Right Candidate

Most park naturalists chose their career because they enjoy working outside near plants and animals. Park naturalists need many skills and abilities to do their jobs. They must be able to work independently. They must be comfortable working in nature. Park naturalists should have good map and geography skills. They should have a good sense of direction. They also should speak and write clearly.

Interests

Park naturalists are interested in nature. They also are interested in science. Science helps them understand and explain nature.

Park naturalists should enjoy teaching others about nature.

Park naturalists often must work alone.

Park naturalists also should enjoy teaching. They want others to understand and appreciate nature. Park naturalists use science to teach others about nature. They encourage people to observe and learn about nature. They show people the best ways to observe plants and animals. They also answer questions about nature.

24

Abilities

Park naturalists must be in good physical condition. They may spend much of their days hiking and working in their parks. They should be able to be physically active for several hours without getting tired.

Park naturalists must be independent. They often work alone. They must be able to set and keep their own schedules.

Park naturalists should work well with people. They may spend a great deal of time working with the public. For example, they may have to give park visitors directions or help visitors who become lost. Park naturalists should be patient and respectful when they work with visitors of all ages.

Skills

Park naturalists must be able to perform a variety of outdoor skills. These may include hiking, canoeing, rock climbing, tree climbing, and swimming. These activities help park naturalists observe nature and assist park visitors. These skills also help park naturalists maintain parks.

Park naturalists need good communication skills. They must be able to express themselves clearly to help others understand nature. They also must be good listeners. This helps park naturalists understand questions.

Park naturalists also must be patient. They often do research by observing patterns in nature. They must observe these patterns over long periods of time. For example, park naturalists may track bird populations over the course of a year. They may count the birds at several different times during the year. They must be patient to do this kind of research.

Technical Skills

Park naturalists need good mathematical skills. They use mathematics to keep track of plant and animal populations. They also use mathematics to create graphs and charts to show trends in nature.

Park naturalists should enjoy working with animals.

Skills

Workplace Skills   Yes / No

Resources:
Assign use of time . . . . ✓ ☐
Assign use of money . . . . ✓ ☐
Assign use of material and facility resources . . . . ✓ ☐
Assign use of human resources . . . . ✓ ☐

Interpersonal Skills:
Take part as a member of a team . . . . ✓ ☐
Teach others . . . . ✓ ☐
Serve clients/customers . . . . ✓ ☐
Show leadership . . . . ✓ ☐
Work with others to arrive at a decision . . . . . ☐ ✓
Work with a variety of people . . . . ✓ ☐

Information:
Acquire and judge information . . . . ✓ ☐
Understand and follow legal requirements . . . . ✓ ☐
Organize and maintain information . . . . . . ✓ ☐
Understand and communicate information . . . . ✓ ☐
Use computers to process information . . . . . ✓ ☐

Systems:
Identify, understand, and work with systems . . . . ✓ ☐
Understand environmental, social, political, economic,
   or business systems . . . . ✓ ☐
Oversee and correct system performance . . . . ✓ ☐
Improve and create systems . . . . ☐ ✓

Technology:
Select technology . . . . ✓ ☐
Apply technology to task . . . . ✓ ☐
Maintain and troubleshoot technology . . . . . ✓ ☐

Foundation Skills

Basic Skills:
Read . . . . ✓ ☐
Write . . . . ✓ ☐
Do arithmetic and math . . . . ✓ ☐
Speak and listen . . . . ✓ ☐

Thinking Skills:
Learn . . . . ✓ ☐
Reason . . . . ✓ ☐
Think creatively . . . . ✓ ☐
Make decisions . . . . ✓ ☐
Solve problems . . . . ✓ ☐

Personal Qualities:
Take individual responsibility . . . . ✓ ☐
Have self-esteem and self-management . . . . . ✓ ☐
Be sociable . . . . ✓ ☐
Be fair, honest, and sincere . . . . ✓ ☐

Park naturalists need good research skills. They should read well. They often must read books and magazines about subjects they are researching. Park naturalists also must have good library skills. This helps them find the materials they need for their research.

Park naturalists need computer skills to perform research on the Internet. They must know how to find sources of information on the Internet. Some park naturalists are in charge of Internet sites. They need computer skills to maintain these sites.

Park naturalists need good writing skills. Many park naturalists write books, magazine articles, or newspaper articles. Others write government reports about nature. These reports often include the park naturalists' research. Governments may use these reports to pass laws that concern nature.

Chapter 4

Preparing for the Career

Most park naturalists earn a bachelor's degree in a scientific field. They take a variety of science classes to prepare themselves for the career.

High School Education

High school students who want to be park naturalists should take science courses. Courses that focus on nature are most helpful. These include biology and ecology. Biology is the study of living things. Ecology is the study of relationships between plants and animals in the environment. Students also should take English and speech classes. These classes help students develop communication skills.

High school students can prepare for careers as park naturalists by attending science camps.

31

Students can learn through other activities. They may gain public speaking skills by taking part in drama classes or school plays. They also can join clubs that involve nature. These include bird-watching clubs or scouting clubs. Students may attend outdoor camps. They may even serve as camp counselors. Counselors are in charge of younger campers. This work helps students gain leadership skills.

Post-Secondary Education

College students who want to be park naturalists should earn a bachelor's degree in a natural science. Many park naturalists earn their degrees in biology or ecology. Some universities and colleges offer specialized degrees in areas such as wildlife management and forestry.

Students may serve as volunteers at local parks or nature centers. Volunteers offer to do jobs without pay. Student volunteers can learn about tasks park naturalists perform. They may even work with experienced park naturalists who can advise them about their careers.

Students may want to be volunteers at local parks or nature centers.

Some college and university students join the National Association for Interpretation (NAI). This organization includes many people who work in natural sciences. Some NAI members are park naturalists. Others work at places such as zoos, museums, historical sites, and aquariums. The NAI offers inexpensive memberships to students.

Finding Jobs

Many college graduates find jobs through contacts they make while in college. For example, ecology students spend a great deal of time working with professionals outdoors. These professionals may know of job openings. They may help the students find jobs.

Other graduates check job listings in magazines, newspapers, and on the Internet. NAI publishes a newsletter that helps its members find jobs. Graduates send resumés to different employers. Resumés are documents that include information about students' education and experience. Employers use resumés to decide who to interview for jobs.

Some students do not look for jobs after they earn a bachelor's degree. They continue their education instead. These students earn a master's degree. They may earn this degree in areas such as environmental science and wildlife management. Park naturalists with a

Students preparing for careers as naturalists should meet and talk to working naturalists.

master's degree may find jobs with more responsibilities.

Continuing Education

Park naturalists continue learning after they graduate. They keep up with new information and trends in their field. They take classes and read professional journals and magazines to do this.

Federal and state government agencies conduct workshops that can help park naturalists continue their education. For example, professional associations may teach classes on pollution. The U.S. Forest Service may conduct classes on how to maintain public trails in parks.

Professional organizations such as the NAI hold meetings and workshops for park naturalists. These are good opportunities for naturalists to get together and discuss ideas. These meetings and workshops help park naturalists keep up with new information in their field.

Park naturalists may take classes on water pollution.

Chapter 5

The Market

About 10,000 naturalists work in the United States today. This includes park naturalists and naturalists who work at zoos, museums, aquariums, and historical sites. Between 5,000 and 6,000 people in Canada work as naturalists. Some naturalists find jobs in other countries. Many work at wildlife preserves in Central America and Africa.

Salary

Most full-time park naturalists in the United States earn between $16,000 and $70,000 per year. Their average salary is about $44,000. Park naturalists in Canada earn between $8,500 and $56,300 per year. Their average salary is about $27,000.

Naturalists work in places such as zoos and aquariums.

Park naturalists' salaries depend on their education and experience. Their salaries also depend on where they work and the kind of work they do. Park naturalists at large parks usually make more money than those who work at small parks.

Job Outlook

The job outlook for park naturalists in the United States and Canada is average. The number of full-time jobs for naturalists is slowly growing. Governments and private tour companies are creating new parks and wildlife refuges in these countries.

Many people seek jobs as park naturalists. This creates a great deal of competition for available jobs.

Advancement Opportunities

Park naturalists may advance as they gain experience. They may gain more responsibilities. They may become supervisors. Supervisors oversee other park naturalists.

Park naturalists must be able to perform many different tasks.

Some park naturalists become park directors. These people handle administrative tasks. They create schedules, plan events, and work with employees. Park directors make more money than park naturalists. But they also spend more time indoors.

Related Careers

Naturalists work in many settings. Some work in zoos. These naturalists care for plants and animals. They decide what foods animals eat. They may design environments for plants and animals.

Other naturalists work at aquariums, museums, and historical sites. These naturalists are in charge of many different natural exhibits. They also teach the public about nature.

Forestry and conservation officers receive training similar to park naturalists' training. These officers enforce laws that affect nature. For example, they prevent people from hunting illegally. Others make sure people do not cut down trees illegally.

Naturalists at zoos may feed the animals.

Words to Know

biology (bye-OL-uh-jee)—the study of living things

ecology (ee-KOL-uh-jee)—the study of the relationships between plants and animals in the environment

endangered species (en-DAYN-jurd SPEE-sheez)—a type of plant or animal in danger of dying out

habitat (HAB-uh-tat)—the natural place and conditions in which a plant or animal lives

interpret (in-TUR-prit)—to explain scientific information about nature through words and stories people can easily understand

research (REE-surch)—the close study of a subject

resumé (RE-zuh-may)—a written summary of a person's experience, job skills, and education

volunteer (vol-uhn-TIHR)—a person who offers to do a job without pay

To Learn More

Burby, Liza N. *A Day in the Life of a Park Ranger.* The Kids' Career Library. New York: PowerKids Press, 1999.

Cosgrove, Holli, ed. *Career Discovery Encyclopedia. Vol. 5.* Chicago: Ferguson Publishing, 2000.

Eberts, Marjorie. *Nature.* VGM's Career Portraits. Lincolnwood, Ill.: VGM Career Horizons, 1997.

Farr, J. Michael and LaVerne Ludden. *Best Jobs for the 21st Century.* Indianapolis: Jist Works, 1999.

Flanagan, Alice K. *Exploring Parks with Ranger Dockett.* Our Neighborhood. New York: Children's Press, 1997.

Useful Addresses

National Association for Interpretation
P.O. Box 2246
Fort Collins, CO 80522

National Park Service
1849 C Street NW
Washington, DC 20240

Parks Canada National Office
25 Eddy Street
Hull, QC K1A OM5
Canada

Internet Sites

Environmental and Conservation Technologies
http://www.hrdc-drhc.gc.ca/JobFutures/english/
    volume2/c640/c640.htm

National Association for Interpretation
http://www.interpnet.com

National Recreation & Park Association
http://www.nrpa.org

**Occupational Outlook Handbook—Foresters
    and Conservation Scientists**
http://www.bls.gov/oco/ocos048.htm

Parks Canada
http://parkscanada.pch.gc.ca/parks/main_e.htm

Index